MY FRIEND has Allergies

BY NICOLA EDWARDS

Chrysalis Children's Books

First published in the UK in 2004 by

Chrysalis Children's Books
An imprint of Chrysalis Books Group
The Chrysalis Building, Bramley Road
London W10 6SP

ISBN 1 84458 097 0

British Library Cataloguing in Publication Data for this book is available from the British Library.

Editorial Manager: Joyce Bentley
Editors: Joe Fullman and Jon Richards
Designers: Ed Simkins and Ben Ruocco
Photographer: Michael Wicks
Picture researcher: Lorna Ainger
Illustrations: Hardlines Ltd
Consultant: Dr Sue Mann

Produced by Tall Tree Ltd.

The photographer and publishers would like to thank James Corcut, Alex Parker, Dominic Keene, Ethel Parker, Angela Corcut and Miles Gray for their help in preparing this book.

Picture acknowledgments:
Alamy/Phototake Inc: 23
Science Photo Library: 28t, Dr Jeremy Burgess 7t, Bsip Edwige 11, Dr. H.C. Robinson 8l, Davis Scharf 27b, Mark Thomas 13t, b
Still Pictures: Jans Peter Lahall 27t

Printed in China

10 9 8 7 6 5 4 3 2 1

Contents

*Words in **bold** are explained in the glossary on page 30.*

My friend Paul

Hello! I'm Michael and this is my friend Paul. We've been friends since I started at our school. The teacher asked Paul to look after me when I was new and he made me feel very welcome. He was easy to talk to, especially when we found out that we both like a lot of the same things. Our favourite hobbies are swimming, playing football, reading, playing computer games, singing and playing guitar – we want to be in a band one day.

On my first day at school, I brought in some sweets to share with everyone in my class. Paul told me he couldn't eat any of the sweets because he has a nut **allergy**. It's very serious, because he could be very ill if he ate any nuts. Paul's also allergic to a medicine called **penicillin** and he gets **hay fever** because he's allergic to **pollen**. He can't have pets at home, either, because they can trigger an **allergic reaction**. Paul has to avoid all the things that could make him ill, but he doesn't let his allergies get in the way of having fun.

Opposite: **Now that he's learnt to avoid substances that he's allergic to, Paul can lead a full and happy life.**

Paul and Michael are good friends. They share a lot of the same hobbies.

ALLERGY FACTS

WHAT DOES IT MEAN?

The word 'allergy' comes from two Greek words: *allos*, which means different or changed, and *ergos*, meaning work or action. An allergic reaction produces changes in the body as it works quickly to fight off a substance which the body thinks is harmful.

What causes allergies?

Paul's doctor knows he is allergic to penicillin, so he gives Paul a different medicine which is safe for him to take.

I like going round to Paul's house. His mum and dad are really nice. When I first met them they told me all about Paul's allergies, so that I would understand why he has to be careful to avoid certain things. They explained that his body would react to things like nuts and pollen that people like me, who aren't allergic, would find completely harmless. Paul's mum told me that the things that can cause allergic reactions are called **allergens**. She said that allergens can be breathed in through the nose and mouth, like house dust, eaten or drunk, like milk, or injected into the body, such as medicines or as a bee or wasp sting.

Paul's dad told me that scientists think the tendency to be allergic to something may be passed on from one family member to another, although they can react to different allergens. Paul and his dad are both allergic to pollen, so they get hay fever in the summer.

Some people are allergic to bee and wasp stings.

ALLERGY FACTS

FOODS TO AVOID

Some of the foods that can cause allergic reactions are:

- cow's milk
- eggs
- fish (such as tuna)
- shellfish (such as prawns)
- peanuts
- tree nuts (such as almonds, Brazil nuts, hazelnuts and walnuts)
- soya
- wheat

Some people are allergic to nuts and milk.

How does the body react?

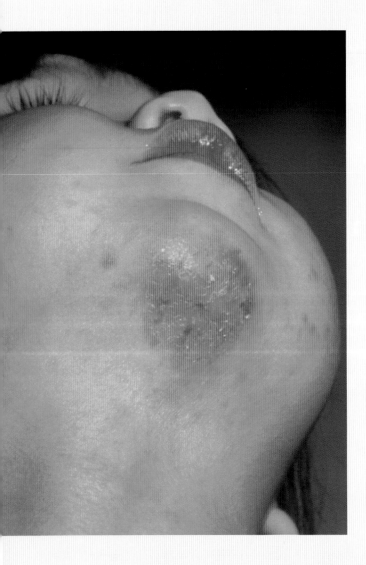

The human body has an **immune system** which protects it against illness. If something that could be harmful, such as a disease-causing **virus**, enters the body, the body's own immune system produces **antibodies** to attack the harmful invader. When a person who is allergic comes into contact with an allergen their body mistakenly thinks the substance is harmful and tries to fight it off. It produces antibodies, which in turn cause the release of chemicals called **histamines** into the blood. These create the **symptoms** of an allergic reaction.

Usually, the symptoms of an allergic reaction begin minutes or even seconds after the person who is allergic has come into contact with the allergen, but sometimes the reaction can happen hours later. Some symptoms are more severe than others. They can vary from a

This child has developed eczema as the result of an allergic reaction. The dry, flaky patches of skin feel itchy and uncomfortable.

wheezy cough, a runny nose and itchy eyes to skin rashes and stomachaches. The most serious reaction is when a person suffers severe **anaphylactic shock**. Their lips and tongue may swell and they may have difficulty breathing. They may vomit or faint. Their life may also be in danger and they will need emergency medical treatment.

These parts of the body (below) can show that an allergic reaction is taking place: eyes (itchy); nose (runny, sneezing); lungs (wheezing, trouble breathing); skin (patches become raised, red, itchy and sore); stomach (ache and vomiting).

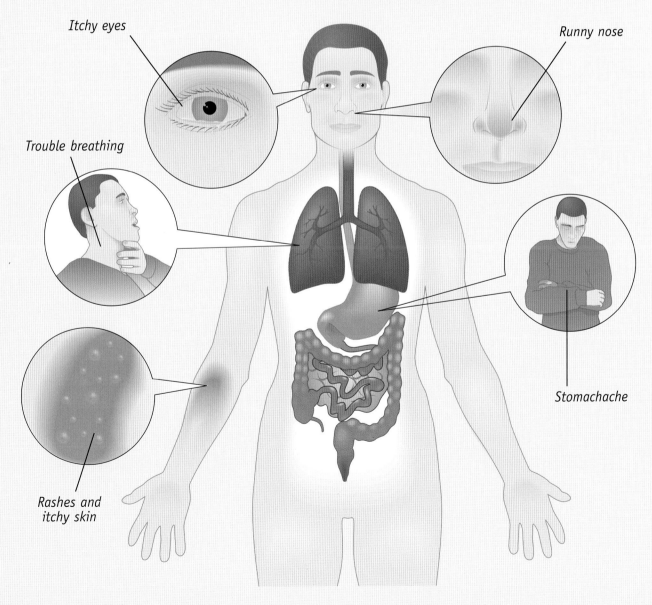

Itchy eyes

Runny nose

Trouble breathing

Stomachache

Rashes and itchy skin

Testing for allergies

'When did you first find out about Paul's allergies?' I asked Paul's mum. 'Well,' she said, 'It was about six years ago. We were staying in a hotel and Paul ate some cereal for breakfast that he hadn't tried before. We found out later that the cereal contained nuts. His skin broke out in a red rash and his body just went sort of floppy. We took Paul to the doctor, who gave him some medicine called an **antihistamine** to make him better.'

'When we got home I had to have a special test to find out which things I'm allergic to,' Paul explained to me. 'The doctor took a sample of my blood and sent it off to a lab so that scientists could find out whether it was just nuts I was allergic to or whether there were other things as well.'

Opposite: **Paul shows Michael photos from the holiday when he first discovered his nut allergy.**

This doctor is checking to find out what the child is allergic to.

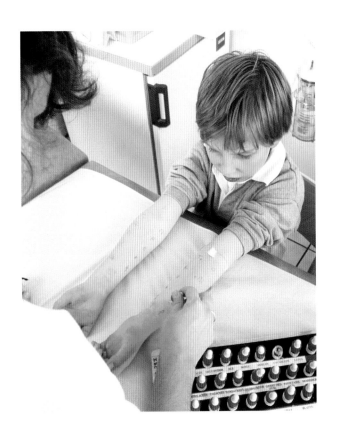

ALLERGY FACTS

TESTS FOR ALLERGIES

There are two main tests which doctors can use to find out what allergens a person will react to:

- Skin prick or scratch test: this is when the doctor puts a tiny amount of a substance on the patient's arm or back and allows it to enter the body by pricking or scratching the skin with a needle. Within about 15 minutes a bump forms on the skin if the patient's body has produced an allergic reaction to the substance.
- Blood test: this is when the doctor takes a sample of the patient's blood and sends it to a laboratory to be tested. The blood is tested with different substances to see whether the patient has antibodies for each substance.

Treating allergies

Paul goes to see his doctor for a checkup to make sure that his allergies are under control.

When Paul's test results came through, he went back to see the doctor with his mum. The doctor told them the results showed that Paul was allergic to nuts, penicillin and pollen, and that pets would also trigger an allergic reaction. 'Doctor Miller told us that there is no cure for allergies, so the most important thing to do is to avoid coming into contact with anything I might have a reaction to,' Paul explained. 'That's right,' said Paul's mum. 'The doctor said if we weren't totally sure that something was safe, it wasn't worth the risk of eating it.'

'The doctor said I'd have to carry a special medicine called **epinephrine** around with me in case I ever had a bad allergic reaction,' Paul told me. 'That's what's inside the **EpiPen** that I take to school. The doctor showed mum and me how the EpiPen works and gave us one without a needle or medicine so that we could practise how to use one safely.'

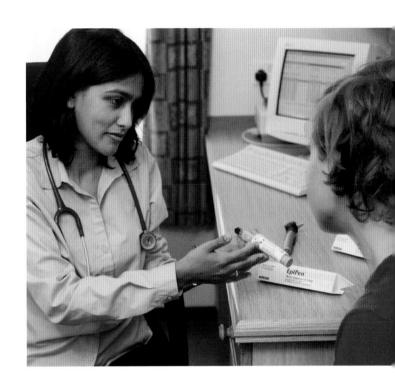

This doctor is showing a patient how to use an EpiPen.

ALLERGY FACTS

USING EPIPENS

Epinephrine is given in an emergency, if someone is showing signs of having an anaphylactic shock. It treats the symptoms by reducing swelling and strengthening the heartbeat, and allows the patient to breathe more easily. An EpiPen can be used by people who are not medically trained to treat someone who is showing the symptoms of an anaphylactic shock.

EpiPens are designed to be easy and quick to use.

Paul's cousin

Paul takes Michael to meet his cousin Jake.

One day Paul was very excited when he came into school. He told me that his cousin Jake was going to be moving to the area where we live. When he'd settled into his new home, Paul took me to meet him. 'Jake has allergies, too, but they're not the same as mine,' Paul told me. I noticed that Jake's house had wooden floors rather than carpets, and wooden blinds instead of curtains covering the windows.

Jake must have his inhaler, or 'puffer', near him at all times.

'That's because I'm allergic to **house dust mites**,' Jake told me when I met him. 'They bring on my **asthma**, so we have to keep the house as free from dust as possible. I have to have a special mattress and bedclothes on my bed, too.'

Like Paul, Jake has to take medicine with him all the time, in case he has an allergic reaction. He calls his medicine container a puffer. He can use it to spray medicine into his mouth whenever he starts to feel the symptoms of asthma.

ALLERGY FACTS

CAUSES OF ASTHMA

Asthma is a breathing problem which is often brought on by an allergic reaction. In children, the most common trigger for asthma is the **rhinovirus**, which causes coughs and colds. Other common triggers are:

- air pollution
- cigarette smoke
- exercise
- pets
- pollen
- sudden temperature changes

At Paul's house

Sometimes I go round to Paul's house after school. This week our class is running a cookie stall to raise money for charity. Paul and I are going to make some biscuits to sell on the stall. Paul knows that he has to avoid anything that might contain nuts or have come into contact with nuts when it was being made. He has to be careful because, even if he touches a nut or accidentally eats a tiny amount, it could trigger an allergic reaction.

Paul's really cool because he doesn't complain about having allergies. I think there are times when I'd feel a bit fed up if I had to be so careful about what I ate. For instance, at Halloween, Paul and I go trick-or-treating with our friends. Before Paul can eat any of the sweets or chocolates we're given, his mum and dad help him check that none of them contains nuts. If they're not sure what the sweets contain, then Paul cannot eat any of them.

Opposite: **Paul and Michael make biscuits to sell at school. They make sure that all the ingredients they use are nut-free.**

Paul must be careful not to eat any nuts or anything that might contain even the smallest trace of nuts.

ALLERGY FACTS

PEANUT ALLERGIES

An allergy to peanuts is one of the most common food allergies. It affects one in every 70 children. It can take just a thousandth of a peanut to trigger a reaction in someone who is allergic to peanuts.

Going shopping

Paul's mum has to read packaging carefully when she goes shopping to make sure she doesn't buy products that contain nuts.

When Paul and his parents go shopping to the supermarket, they read the product labels carefully to make sure the food they buy is nut-free. Paul says you can't tell just by looking at something, because sometimes the nuts used are ground into a powder, so they are too small to see. He has learnt about the different words which can mean that a product has nuts in it. 'Sometimes it will say groundnuts instead of peanuts in a list of ingredients,' he told me. Sometimes the label says 'may contain nut traces' because the product has been made in a factory where nuts are used to make other things.

Paul told me he was surprised by some of the products that are made with nuts. It's not just foods and drinks that can contain nuts or that might be made with oil from nuts. Nuts are also used as ingredients in some skin-care products, shampoos and conditioners.

Traces of nuts can be found in a surprising number of products, including sunscreen, shampoo and skin creams.

ALLERGY FACTS

HIDDEN NUTS

Food products that may contain unexpected or 'hidden' sources of nuts include cakes, biscuits, chocolate, ice cream, salad dressings and breakfast cereals. Peanut oil is even an ingredient in some creams used to treat the symptoms of eczema. The latin word *arachis* in the list of ingredients on a product sold in a chemists is a sign that the product contains peanuts.

At school

Sometimes, Paul helps the kitchen staff to clear away and talks to them about his allergies.

Paul takes a packed lunch to school every day. That way he knows exactly what he's eating and that everything is nut-free. He keeps his food in a lunchbox until he's ready to eat it, so he knows it can't have been in contact with any nuts. Before Paul sits down, one of the kitchen staff wipes the table with a damp cloth to make sure it's clean.

Paul takes a packed lunch into school and eats it with Michael.

There are several children in our school who have allergies and most are allergic to nuts. Our headteacher, Mrs Allen, told parents that the school is a nut-free zone. That means that no nuts are allowed in the school. The kitchen staff don't use nuts in any meals and the children who take packed lunches to school are not allowed to bring in anything containing nuts.

ALLERGY FACTS

HELPING WITH ALLERGIES

Four out of ten schoolchildren have one or more allergies. There may be children in your class who are allergic to something. You can help them by knowing about their allergies and making sure you don't bring anything containing an allergen into school. See pages 22–23 to find out about the symptoms your friends might have during an allergic reaction and how you could help them in an emergency.

In an emergency

Paul's headmistress has an EpiPen in her office in case of emergencies.

However careful Paul is to avoid nuts, he may accidentally come into contact with them, so it's important that we all know how to help him in an emergency. Last year Paul did have an allergic reaction at school. Someone in our class brought in some chocolate cake. Paul asked if the cake was nut-free and our friend said it was. He didn't know that some chocolate is made with peanut oil.

Paul had only had a few bites of the cake when he said he didn't feel right. I ran to the staffroom to find our teacher. She knew what to do straight away. She brought Paul's EpiPen and gave Paul an injection with it. Then she phoned for an ambulance, and explained about Paul's allergy and what he had eaten. Luckily Paul's symptoms went away and he was fine. He had to stay at the hospital for a few hours in case the symptoms came back, but they didn't and he was able to come to school again the next day.

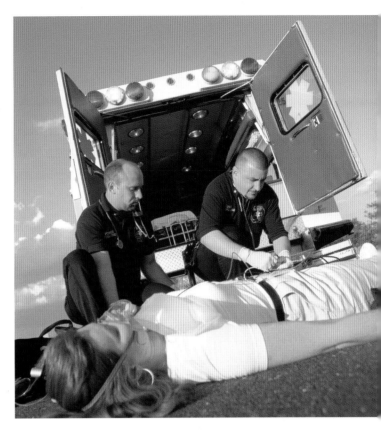

This ambulance crew is treating a person who has suffered from an allergic reaction.

ALLERGY FACTS

HELPING IN AN EMERGENCY

If someone is having an extreme allergic reaction (called an anaphylactic shock) they need help straight away. Call an adult who will be able to use an EpiPen to give the person an injection of epinephrine. Then phone for an ambulance or ask someone else to do it for you.

At Michael's house

Paul's mum explains what to do to help Paul if he shows signs of an allergic reaction.

Sometimes Paul comes to my house for a sleepover. We watch a film and stay up for ages, chatting. We have a cat called Kevin at home, but we make sure he doesn't come near Paul because he is allergic to cats. Mum and Dad make sure the house is as clean as possible because Kevin's hairs get everywhere!

When Paul's mum drops him off she gives us an EpiPen just in case Paul needs it. Paul's mum told my mum that, to give Paul an injection, she would

*Paul enjoys a nut-free
meal at Michael's house.*

need to take the cap off and then hold the EpiPen in place for at least ten seconds.

When Mum or Dad cooks us a meal, they always make sure that they use ingredients that are completely nut-free. Home-made pizzas are our favourite! Paul's allergies don't stop him from enjoying himself and having fun. He said that he feels comfortable at our house because he knows he could tell us if he felt an allergic reaction was starting, and we would know what to do.

ALLERGY FACTS

PET ALLERGIES

Cats, dogs and other pets such as birds are a source of allergens. Tiny pieces of skin, fur or feathers, called **dander**, are carried in the air and can create a reaction in someone who is allergic.

At the weekend

Paul and his family like going out at the weekend and sometimes they invite me along, too. Paul's mum and dad take a picnic with them, so they are sure that Paul will be able to eat safely.

Paul's mum and dad have to choose where to picnic carefully in the summer, because that's when Paul and his dad get hay fever. It makes them sneeze and their ears, noses and throats feel itchy. They are allergic to pollen, the powdery material made by plants which is carried on the wind. They prefer to sit on the lawn of the rose garden of our local park, because areas where there are tall grasses and trees make their symptoms worse. Both Paul and his dad take a medicine that keeps their hay fever symptoms under control, so that they can enjoy the summer.

Opposite: **Paul and Michael help to pack a nut-free picnic.**

These grasses make small, dry pollen. This is light enough to be carried by the wind and can trigger allergy symptoms in people who have hay fever.

ALLERGY FACTS

POLLEN

This photo of pollen particles has been magnified many times. Pollen is needed for flowering plants to reproduce. Some larger, heavier pollens are carried by bees from one plant to another. Other lighter pollens are blown in the wind. A **pollen count** measures the amount of pollen contained in a sample of air. A high pollen count means that people with hay fever are more likely to experience allergic symptoms.

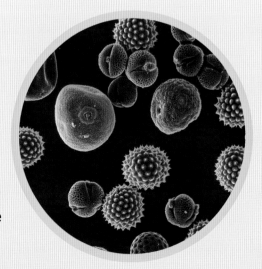

Questions people ask

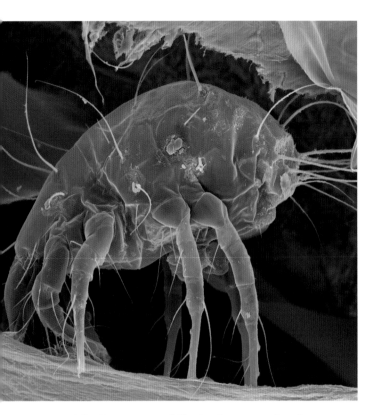

This is a magnified picture of a house dust mite.

Q. **Can you outgrow a food allergy?**
A. Yes, people often do grow out of their allergies to some foods, such as milk and eggs. But it seems that allergies to other foods, such as nuts and shellfish, can last a lifetime.

Q. **Is there a cure for allergies?**
A. Scientists haven't yet found a cure for allergies, but research is going on all the time. At the moment, the best way to prevent allergic symptoms from developing is to avoid coming into contact with the allergens such as nuts or pollen or house dust mites that would trigger a reaction.

Q. **How do I know if I'm allergic to something?**
A. You would experience the symptoms of an allergic reaction after coming into contact with an allergen. For example, if you were allergic to a certain food, you might develop an itch or a rash, or start to wheeze after eating it. If you were allergic to pets, you might sneeze, your eyes might start to itch and you might feel a tightness in your chest when you came into contact with a cat or a dog.

Michael knows how to help Paul if he ever has an allergic reaction.

If you think you might be allergic to something, talk to someone you trust at home or at school. You will be able to see a doctor who can do tests to find out if you have any allergies.

Cigarette smoke can trigger allergic reactions in some people.

Q. Can an allergic reaction kill you?

A. If an allergic reaction turns into an anaphylactic shock, it can be life-threatening. That is why it is important for people who are at risk to carry life-saving medicine with them, so that they can be treated even before an ambulance arrives. It's also important that people know how to help someone who is having an allergic reaction.

Q. How can I help my friend who's allergic?

A. Find out about your friend's allergy and its symptoms, and the allergens he or she needs to avoid. Help your friend to keep well clear of these allergens. For example, if you have a pet, make sure it doesn't come near your friend, or, if your friend has a nut allergy, remember not to bring anything that contains nuts into school. Make sure you know how to help your friend in an emergency.

Q. What should I do if my friend is having an allergic reaction?

A. Your friend may need to be given the medicine epinephrine immediately. Keep calm and alert someone who will be able to give your friend an injection with an EpiPen. Make sure that you or someone else phones for an ambulance, giving information about your friend's allergy and describing what has happened to trigger the allergic reaction. When the ambulance is on its way, call your friend's mum, dad or other carer to let them know what has happened.

Q. Are there any activities that people with allergies should avoid?

A. People who have allergies need to avoid coming into contact with the allergens that may trigger their allergic reaction. They may need to carry medicine with them for use in an emergency, such as an inhaler or an EpiPen. Apart from that, people with allergies can be as active and have as much fun as any other person.

Glossary

allergens The things that can trigger an allergic reaction in a person who has an allergy. Allergens can enter the body by being eaten, touched, breathed in or injected into the body.

allergic reaction The changes that happen in the body when the immune system responds to protect the body from what it wrongly believes to be a harmful substance.

allergy The immune system's response to a certain allergen which produces the symptoms of an allergic reaction.

anaphylactic shock A severe allergic reaction which must be treated with an injection of epinephrine.

antibodies The chemicals that are produced by the body to fight off illness or infection.

antihistamine A type of medicine which is used to treat the symptoms of a mild allergic reaction, such as a skin rash.

asthma A breathing problem which happens when air passages in the lungs become narrower, often as the result of an allergic reaction.

dander Tiny pieces of skin, hair and feathers from animals to which some people are allergic.

epinephrine The medicine (also known as adrenaline) which is used to treat the symptoms of a severe allergic reaction.

EpiPen A device containing a dose of epinephrine. An EpiPen can be used in an emergency to inject medicine into a patient who is having a severe allergic reaction.

hay fever An illness which is caused by an allergy to pollen.

histamines Chemicals made by the body in response to an allergen which create the symptoms of an allergic reaction.

house dust mites Tiny creatures that live in house dust and can trigger allergic illnesses such as asthma.

immune system The system that protects the body from illness and infection.

penicillin A medicine which can be used to treat some illnesses and infections. Some people are allergic to penicillin.

pollen The dust-like material which is made by flowering plants and is needed for them to reproduce. Hay fever sufferers have an allergy to pollen.

pollen count The number of grains of pollen in a certain amount of air.

rhinovirus A virus that affects the nose, creating the symptoms of a cold.

symptoms The ways in which someone shows that they may have a particular problem or illness. For example, coughs, sneezes and a sore throat are symptoms of a cold.

virus Tiny germs which cause illnesses when they enter the body and multiply inside it.

Useful organisations

HERE ARE SOME ORGANISATIONS YOU MIGHT LIKE TO CONTACT FOR MORE INFORMATION ABOUT ALLERGIES

ALLERGY UK
Allergy Helpline: 020 8303 8583
Email: info@allergyuk.org
www.allergyfoundation.com

THE ANAPHYLAXIS CAMPAIGN
PO Box 275
Farnborough
Hampshire GU14 6SX
Tel: 01252 542 029
www.anaphylaxis.org.uk

THE BRITISH DIETETIC ASSOCIATION
5th Floor, Charles House
148–149 Great Charles Street
Queensway
Birmingham B3 3HT
Tel: 0121 200 8080
Email: info@bda.uk.com
www.bda.uk.com

NATIONAL ASTHMA CAMPAIGN
Asthma Helpline: 08457 010 203
www.asthma.org.uk

NATIONAL ECZEMA SOCIETY
Hill House
Highgate Hill
London N19 5NA
Tel: 020 7281 3553
Helpline: 0870 241 3604
www.eczema.org

MEDIC ALERT FOUNDATION
1 Bridge Wharf
156 Caledonian Road
London N1 9UU
Tel: 020 7833 3034

Index